Counting Up

A Kindness-a-Day
Sefirat HaOmer
Workbook for Kids

Sari Kopitnikoff

Ideastrator
Press

Counting Up
An Interactive *Sefirat HaOmer* Workbook for Kids

Copyright ©2023 by Sari Kopitnikoff

ISBN 979-8-9851605-5-0, paperback

Published by Ideastrator Press, New Jersey

The author welcomes feedback at sari@thatjewishmoment.com.

Dedicated to

Shoshanna Clementine

May your memory
be for a blessing.

"Teach us to count our days
so we may gain a heart of
wisdom." —Psalms 90:12

With infinite love
from your parents,
grandparents, sisters,
aunts and uncles,
and all of our family and friends

In honor of

Daryl Bain

**United Jewish Center
Religious School Director**

With thanks,

Cantor Penny Kessler

Senior Clergy
United Jewish Center
Danbury, Connecticut

In loving memory of

Laura Stock Vinegar

Leah Bat Nechemiah HaKohen

Through her warmth and wisdom, she was
a giver, like no other—to her family, friends,
community, and even strangers.

May the kindness that results
from this book elevate her soul.

In memory of

Mrs. Evelyn Silverberg Hoffman

Chava bat Shmuel

May her *neshama*
have an *aliyah*

In loving memory of

Yoseph Itzkovich

Yoseph ben Itzchak v'Rivka

He was the kindest
Abba and Sabba to us
and is greatly missed

May the kindness that results
from this book
elevate his soul

With love,
the Berkovitz Family

In honor of

**Alexandra,
Elizabeth,
and Jared**

With love
from Hoboken, NJ!

Shana Lee

In loving memory of

Batsheva Stadlen

*Batsheva Chaya
bat Noam Yigal V'Rina*

who led her life
with kindness,
making it the cool, beautiful,
and fun thing to do.

**Krieger Schechter
Day School**

is a proud sponsor
of this wonderful program

Introduction

We're often counting down.
"5 days till my birthday!"
"Only 2 weeks until vacation."
"3 minutes left..."

But *Sefirat HaOmer*, the period of counting between *Pesach* and *Shavuot*, is unique. Instead of counting down until the day that celebrates when we received the Torah long ago, we count up. Our Sages explain it's because we're focused on growing and becoming better people.

That's why this book is called *Counting Up*. *Sefirat HaOmer* is a time when we can focus on becoming better versions of ourselves, specifically in the area of kindness. And this book is here to help you do just that.

Use this book to remind you to count the *Omer* each day, and also to help you become an even kinder person.

Each week focuses on one area of kindness. Complete the various challenges, and then, at the end of each week, use the reflection page to look back on your accomplishments.

Wishing you success in your counting up. And I hope you have fun in the process!

A Few Notes

Shabbat and **Yom Tov**: When it's *Shabbat* or *Yom Tov*, you can skip the writing/drawing part and just think about the prompt instead, or discuss it with a family member or friend.

Night and Day: The Jewish day begins at nightfall. Many count the *Omer* at night, while others count during the day. In this book, several of the pages suggest doing something "today." If you count at night, realize you have until the following night to do the activity.

Counting Variations: There are various traditions about the actual counting. Some say *LaOmer* and some say *BaOmer*. This book uses *LaOmer* but you can find out what your community does.

Calendar: At the top of each counting page is the Hebrew date as well as any minor holiday that falls out on that day. *Yom HaShoah*, *Yom HaZikaron*, *Yom HaAtzmaut*, and *Yom Yerushalayim* are included on the Hebrew dates they usually fall out on, though they are occasionally moved (ex: to not interfere with *Shabbat*).

God's name: This book contains the name of God. Please treat it with appropriate respect.

Questions, thoughts, comments, or suggestions? Email me at sari@thatjewishmoment.com.

Acknowledgements

This project began when a colleague, Toby Goldfisher Kaplowitz, put out a query asking if such a book existed: a *Sefirat HaOmer* project where students could count each day and be inspired to develop their kindness. I wasn't aware of one, but I loved the idea. I wanted to try to make it happen.

The deadline was impending. I had just a few days to make it. And without the following people, you would not be holding this book. Thank you all for your guidance, suggestions, and feedback: Amy Ariel, Lisa Bernstein, July Blair, Michael Cohen, Nina Cusner, Arnie Draiman, Sapphira Edgarde, Wendy Goldberg, Joey Heyman, Robin Kahn, Helene Kornsgold, Rachel Mann, Stephanie Marshall, Maya Resnikoff, Mariel Seta, Anna Yolkut, and Rebeccah Yussman.

And a big thank you to all the generous sponsors of this book, who allowed this project to happen. Reader, I invite you to please take a look at the dedication pages to honor the people involved.

Counting

Before counting each day, many recite the following blessing:

Baruch Atta	בָּרוּךְ אַתָּה
Adonai	אֲדֹנָי
Eloheinu	אֱלֹהֵינוּ
Melech HaOlam	מֶלֶךְ הָעוֹלָם
Asher Kideshanu BeMitzvotav	אֲשֶׁר קִדְּשָׁנוּ בְּמִצְוֹתָיו
VeTzivanu Al Sefirat HaOmer.	וְצִוָּנוּ עַל סְפִירַת הָעֹמֶר:

Blessed are You
Adonai
our God
Ruler of the world
Who blessed us with *mitzvot*
and commanded us to count the *Omer*.

Week 1

Be kind to yourself.

An important idea in Judaism is, "Love your neighbor like you love yourself." Before we start thinking about being kind to others, we have to make sure we're kind to ourselves. This week, let's explore how to do that.

Day 1

Today is Day One of
the Omer.

הַיּוֹם יוֹם אֶחָד לָעֹמֶר:

What are three things you love about yourself?

 I counted up today!

Day 2

Today is Two Days of
the Omer.

הַיּוֹם שְׁנֵי יָמִים לָעֹמֶר:

Practicing gratitude can help you love yourself even more.
What are three things in your life you feel grateful for?

 I counted up today!

Day 3

Today is Three Days
of the Omer.

הַיּוֹם שְׁלשָׁה יָמִים לָעֹמֶר:

What's something you enjoy doing? Write or draw it below,
and at some point today, try to do that thing.

I counted up today!

Day 4

Today is Four Days of
the Omer.

הַיּוֹם אַרְבָּעָה יָמִים
לָעֹמֶר:

What's your favorite song? Jot it down below. And at some
point today, listen to it, sing it, play it on an instrument, or
dance to it.

 I counted up today!

Day 5

Today is Five Days of
the Omer.

הַיּוֹם חֲמִשָּׁה יָמִים לָעֹמֶר:

Practice mindfulness. Spend a few minutes just focusing
on the moment. You can concentrate on your breathing, or
use your senses to notice your surroundings. Afterwards,
record how it felt.

 I counted up today!

Day 6

Today is Six Days of
the Omer.

הַיּוֹם שִׁשָּׁה יָמִים לָעֹמֶר:

Sometimes, it helps to hear from people who love us. Ask a
friend or family member what is something they love about
you. Record it below.

 I counted up today!

Day 7

Today is Seven Days,
which are One Week
of the Omer.

הַיּוֹם שִׁבְעָה יָמִים, שֶׁהֵם
שָׁבוּעַ אֶחָד לָעֹמֶר:

Make your bedtime routine a bit more enjoyable. Read a
book, spend some time journaling, or go to bed a little
early. Below, write or draw what you'll do.

 I counted up today!

Week 1:
Time to Reflect

Flip back and skim the pages from this past week. What were your highlights? What was the biggest challenge? What do you hope to bring with you into the future weeks? Jot down some thoughts below.

Week 2

Be kind to family and friends.

Once we can be kind to ourselves, we can begin to reach out to the people in our closest circles. Let's now explore how we can practice kindness with the important people in our lives.

Day 8

Today is Eight Days,
which are One Week
and One Day of the
Omer.

הַיּוֹם שְׁמוֹנָה יָמִים, שֶׁהֵם
שָׁבוּעַ אֶחָד וְיוֹם אֶחָד
לָעֹמֶר:

A simple way to show kindness is by letting someone know
we're thinking of them. Call a relative or friend just to say
hello. Jot down below who you plan to call and something
kind you can say.

 I counted up today!

Day 9

Today is Nine Days, which are One Week and Two Days of the Omer.

הַיּוֹם תִּשְׁעָה יָמִים, שֶׁהֵם שָׁבוּעַ אֶחָד וּשְׁנֵי יָמִים לָעֹמֶר:

It's kind to help clean! What area in your home can you tidy up? Jot it down below.

 I counted up today!

Day 10

Today is Ten Days,
which are One Week
and Three Days of
the Omer.

הַיּוֹם עֲשָׂרָה יָמִים, שֶׁהֵם
שָׁבוּעַ אֶחָד וּשְׁלֹשָׁה יָמִים
לָעֹמֶר:

What household chore can you help with, even if no one asks you to do it? Draw or write it below. And then, at some point today, try to do the chore!

Day 11

Today is Eleven Days, which are One Week and Four Days of the Omer.

הַיּוֹם אַחַד עָשָׂר יוֹם, שֶׁהֵם שָׁבוּעַ אֶחָד וְאַרְבָּעָה יָמִים לָעֹמֶר:

Imagine getting a letter in the mail from someone who loves you. That would be so kind. Think of someone you can send a note to. What will you write in the card? Jot it down below.

 I counted up today!

Day 12

Yom HaShoah

כ״ז ניסן

Today is Twelve Days, which are One Week and Five Days of the Omer.

הַיּוֹם שְׁנֵים עָשָׂר יוֹם, שֶׁהֵם שָׁבוּעַ אֶחָד וַחֲמִשָּׁה יָמִים לָעֹמֶר:

Choose someone you love. No need to wait till their birthday to give them a gift. Surprise them with something small and fun. It can be something you bake, a craft you design, or a present you buy. Brainstorm below.

 I counted up today!

Day 13

כ״ח ניסן

Today is Thirteen
Days, which are One
Week and Six Days of
the Omer.

הַיּוֹם שְׁלֹשָׁה עָשָׂר יוֹם,
שֶׁהֵם שָׁבוּעַ אֶחָד וְשִׁשָּׁה
יָמִים לָעֹמֶר:

Offer to help out a family member or friend. What are
some things you're good at doing? List them below, and
then think of how you can use one of those skills to help
someone you love.

 I counted up today!

Day 14

Today is Fourteen
Days, which are Two
Weeks of the Omer.

הַיּוֹם אַרְבָּעָה עָשָׂר
יוֹם, שֶׁהֵם שְׁנֵי שָׁבוּעוֹת
לָעֹמֶר:

Leave a kind note of encouragement for someone you care
about. It can be on their mirror, on their desk, or on their
door. What's something you might write? Jot it down below.

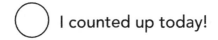 I counted up today!

Week 2:
Time to Reflect

Flip back and skim the pages from this past week. What were your highlights? What was the biggest challenge? What do you hope to bring with you into the future weeks? Write down some thoughts below.

Week 3

Be kind to your community.

An important value in Judaism is being part of a community. This week, let's think of ways you can reach out and lend a hand.

Day 15

Rosh Chodesh

Today is Fifteen Days, which are Two Weeks and One Day of the Omer.

הַיּוֹם חֲמִשָּׁה עָשָׂר יוֹם, שֶׁהֵם שְׁנֵי שָׁבוּעוֹת וְיוֹם אֶחָד לָעֹמֶר:

A huge way to help out others in your community is to donate things you don't need to people who could use them. Think of some books, toys, and clothes you own. What do you no longer need? Write or draw them below, and then find out how you can donate them.

 I counted up today!

Day 16

Rosh Chodesh

Today is Sixteen
Days, which are Two
Weeks and Two Days
of the Omer.

הַיּוֹם שִׁשָּׁה עָשָׂר יוֹם,
שֶׁהֵם שְׁנֵי שָׁבוּעוֹת וּשְׁנֵי
יָמִים לָעֹמֶר:

Is there someone in your community who could use a little extra help? Maybe there's a family with a new baby, someone who has health challenges, or an older person who would appreciate some help or even some company. Jot down your idea below, and then offer to help out for a bit.

 I counted up today!

Day 17

Today is Seventeen Days, which are Two Weeks and Three Days of the Omer.

הַיּוֹם שִׁבְעָה עָשָׂר יוֹם,
שֶׁהֵם שְׁנֵי שָׁבוּעוֹת
וּשְׁלֹשָׁה יָמִים לָעֹמֶר:

Kindness makes the world go round. Offer to do something for someone in your community—for free. For example, you can pull out someone's weeds, bring in someone's mail, or walk their dog. Write or draw your idea below.

 I counted up today!

Day 18

ג׳ אייר ✓

Today is Eighteen
Days, which are Two
Weeks and Four Days
of the Omer.

הַיּוֹם שְׁמוֹנָה עָשָׂר יוֹם,
שֶׁהֵם שְׁנֵי שָׁבוּעוֹת
וְאַרְבָּעָה יָמִים לָעֹמֶר:

Every community has some organizations that do kindness
for people in need. Find out about some of your community's
organizations, and write them down below. Then reach out
to one of them and see how you can help them for a day.

Chari
lleeline

Yad
Leah

Tomchei
Shabbos

 I counted up today!

Day 19

Yom HaZikaron

ד׳ אייר

Today is Nineteen
Days, which are Two
Weeks and Five Days
of the Omer.

הַיּוֹם תִּשְׁעָה עָשָׂר יוֹם,
שֶׁהֵם שְׁנֵי שָׁבוּעוֹת
וַחֲמִשָּׁה יָמִים לָעֹמֶר:

Make some hand-made cards and then deliver them in
your community: to volunteer firefighters, residents of a
retirement home, healthcare workers, or veterans of the
army. They don't need to be fancy cards to bring real smiles
to people's faces. Practice here and make a sample card
below.

 I counted up today!

Day 20

Yom HaAtzmaut

ה׳ אייר

Today is Twenty Days, which are Two Weeks and Six Days of the Omer.

הַיּוֹם עֶשְׂרִים יוֹם, שֶׁהֵם שְׁנֵי שָׁבוּעוֹת וְשִׁשָּׁה יָמִים לָעֹמֶר:

Leave a thank you note and a small treat for a community worker in your community. For example, leave a note on your mailbox for the mail carrier or a card near your trash can for the sanitation workers.

 I counted up today!

Day 21

Today is Twenty-One
Days, which are Three
Weeks of the Omer.

הַיּוֹם אֶחָד וְעֶשְׂרִים יוֹם,
שֶׁהֵם שְׁלֹשָׁה שָׁבוּעוֹת
לָעֹמֶר:

Create a kindness stone! Use permanent markers or paint
to decorate a stone with a kind message, and then leave
it somewhere in your community. Plan out your kindness
stone below.

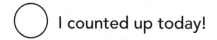 I counted up today!

Week 3:
Time to Reflect

Flip back and skim the pages from this past week. What were your highlights? What was the biggest challenge? What do you hope to bring with you into the future weeks? Jot down some thoughts below.

Week 4

Be kind in your speech.

Your mouth is a wonderful thing. It has the power to make someone's day. These next 7 days, let's think of how we can use the power of speech to bring more kindness into the world.

Day 22

Today is Twenty-Two Days, which are Three Weeks and One Day of the Omer.

הַיּוֹם שְׁנַיִם וְעֶשְׂרִים יוֹם,
שֶׁהֵם שְׁלֹשָׁה שָׁבוּעוֹת
וְיוֹם אֶחָד לָעֹמֶר:

Compliments make people feel really special. Today, what compliment can you give someone? (Tip: Try to praise someone on their personality instead of how they look.) Write it down below, and then remember to give the compliment later.

 I counted up today!

Day 23

Today is Twenty-Three Days, which are Three Weeks and Two Days of the Omer.

הַיּוֹם שְׁלֹשָׁה וְעֶשְׂרִים יוֹם,
שֶׁהֵם שְׁלֹשָׁה שָׁבוּעוֹת
וּשְׁנֵי יָמִים לָעֹמֶר:

While complimenting someone directly is a beautiful kindness, we can also pass the praise along to someone who will care. Think of it as kind tattle telling. For example, tell a friend's parent how great your friend is. Or tell your principal how wonderful your teacher is. Jot down below how you might share someone's praise today with someone who will appreciate hearing it.

 I counted up today!

Day 24

Today is Twenty-Four Days, which are Three Weeks and Three Days of the Omer.

הַיּוֹם אַרְבָּעָה וְעֶשְׂרִים יוֹם, שֶׁהֵם שְׁלֹשָׁה שָׁבוּעוֹת וּשְׁלֹשָׁה יָמִים לָעֹמֶר:

An important phrase to learn to say is, "I was wrong. I'm sorry." (Only if it's true, of course.) Today, look out for an opportunity to apologize. Take some time to think, and then below, jot down anyone you may owe an apology to.

 I counted up today!

Day 25

Today is Twenty-Five Days, which are Three Weeks and Four Days of the Omer.

הַיּוֹם חֲמִשָּׁה וְעֶשְׂרִים יוֹם, שֶׁהֵם שְׁלֹשָׁה שָׁבוּעוֹת וְאַרְבָּעָה יָמִים לָעֹמֶר:

One way to be kinder in our speech is to avoid speaking unkindly about other people. Pick an hour today (and write it down below!) when you can be extra careful to not speak badly about other people.

 I counted up today!

Day 26

Today is Twenty-Six Days, which are Three Weeks and Five Days of the Omer.

הַיּוֹם שִׁשָּׁה וְעֶשְׂרִים יוֹם,
שֶׁהֵם שְׁלֹשָׁה שָׁבוּעוֹת
וַחֲמִשָּׁה יָמִים לָעֹמֶר:

Today, give genuine thanks to someone. It can be for something small ("Thank you for passing me my paper") or something big ("Thank you for teaching me this year and for being so kind and caring.") Write down some ideas below of who you can thank today.

 I counted up today!

Day 27

Today is Twenty-
Seven Days, which
are Three Weeks and
Six Days of the Omer.

הַיּוֹם שִׁבְעָה וְעֶשְׂרִים יוֹם,
שֶׁהֵם שְׁלֹשָׁה שָׁבוּעוֹת
וְשִׁשָּׁה יָמִים לָעֹמֶר:

A surprising way to be kind in our speech is to say... nothing.
Today, when you're chatting with someone, try to do more
listening than talking. Below, see if you can figure out what
the letters SILENT spell if you rearrange them.

 I counted up today!

Day 28

Today is Twenty-Eight
Days, which are Four
Weeks of the Omer.

הַיּוֹם שְׁמוֹנָה וְעֶשְׂרִים
יוֹם, שֶׁהֵם אַרְבָּעָה
שָׁבוּעוֹת לָעֹמֶר:

Often, people ask, "How are you?" to be polite, but
sometimes they don't stick around for the answer. Today,
ask someone how they're doing, and stay around for the
response. Follow up with them about something (like,
"How's your house construction going?" or "Is your cat
feeling better?") Below, write down some other ways to
ask someone how they're doing.

 I counted up today!

Week 4:
Time to Reflect

Flip back and skim the pages from this past week. What were your highlights? What was the biggest challenge? What do you hope to bring with you into the future weeks? Jot down some thoughts below.

Week 5

Be kind in your actions.

"Actions speak louder than words."

How can we be kind without even saying a word? This week, let's explore some ideas to do just that.

Day 29

Today is Twenty-Nine Days, which are Four Weeks and One Day of the Omer.

הַיּוֹם תִּשְׁעָה וְעֶשְׂרִים יוֹם,
שֶׁהֵם אַרְבָּעָה שָׁבוּעוֹת
וְיוֹם אֶחָד לָעֹמֶר:

A simple and small way to show kindness is by holding the door open for someone to walk through. Today, try to do that for someone. And below, draw a picture of someone holding the door open for someone else.

 I counted up today!

Day 30

Today is Thirty Days, which are Four Weeks and Two Days of the Omer.

הַיּוֹם שְׁלֹשִׁים יוֹם, שֶׁהֵם אַרְבָּעָה שָׁבוּעוֹת וּשְׁנֵי יָמִים לָעֹמֶר:

They say smiles are contagious. That sounds like something worth spreading. Today, try to give your full smile: involving your mouth and eyes. See how many people you can give a smile to. And to get you in the mood, fill the space below with smiley faces.

 I counted up today!

Day 31

Today is Thirty-One Days, which are Four Weeks and Three Days of the Omer.

הַיּוֹם אֶחָד וּשְׁלשִׁים יוֹם,
שֶׁהֵם אַרְבָּעָה שָׁבוּעוֹת
וּשְׁלשָׁה יָמִים לָעֹמֶר:

Today, reach out to someone who is sitting or standing alone. Yes, they might need some quiet or want some time to think. But they might also really appreciate you connecting with them. Below, write down how you might feel if someone came to talk to you while you were standing alone.

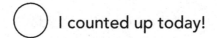 I counted up today!

Day 32

Today is Thirty-Two Days, which are Four Weeks and Four Days of the Omer.

הַיּוֹם שְׁנַיִם וּשְׁלֹשִׁים יוֹם,
שֶׁהֵם אַרְבָּעָה שָׁבוּעוֹת
וְאַרְבָּעָה יָמִים לָעֹמֶר:

We spend a lot of time waiting in line. Today, what if you let the person behind you go ahead of you? Try to look for an opportunity today to do that. Below, write down some examples of when people wait in line.

 I counted up today!

Day 33

Lag BaOmer

י״ח אייר

Today is Thirty-Three Days, which are Four Weeks and Five Days of the Omer.

הַיּוֹם שְׁלֹשָׁה וּשְׁלֹשִׁים יוֹם, שֶׁהֵם אַרְבָּעָה שָׁבוּעוֹת וַחֲמִשָּׁה יָמִים לָעֹמֶר:

Today, give someone a friendly wave. Below, draw a person waving.

 I counted up today!

Day 34

Today is Thirty-Four Days, which are Four Weeks and Six Days of the Omer.

הַיּוֹם אַרְבָּעָה וּשְׁלֹשִׁים יוֹם, שֶׁהֵם אַרְבָּעָה שָׁבוּעוֹת וְשִׁשָּׁה יָמִים לָעֹמֶר:

Giving *tzedakkah* helps people in need. But it also helps us -- as we become kinder people. What are some organizations you can give *tzedakkah* to? Jot some down below, and then pick one to give money to today.

 I counted up today!

Day 35

Today is Thirty-Five Days, which are Five Weeks of the Omer.

הַיּוֹם חֲמִשָּׁה וּשְׁלֹשִׁים יוֹם, שֶׁהֵם חֲמִשָּׁה שָׁבוּעוֹת לָעֹמֶר:

Leave an anonymous positive note somewhere that will bring smiles. For example, leave a note inside a book at the library or in chalk on the sidewalk. Write down some ideas below of what you might write and where you might put the message.

 I counted up today!

Week 5:
Time to Reflect

Flip back and skim the pages from this past week. What were your highlights? What was the biggest challenge? What do you hope to bring with you into the future weeks? Jot down some thoughts below.

Week 6

Be kind to nature.

These last few weeks, we focused on being kind to people. Did you know there are *mitzvot* related to being kind to animals and nature? After all, it's up to us to care for the environment that we inhabit.

Day 36

Today is Thirty-Six Days, which are Five Weeks and One Day of the Omer.

הַיּוֹם שִׁשָּׁה וּשְׁלשִׁים יוֹם, שֶׁהֵם חֲמִשָּׁה שָׁבוּעוֹת וְיוֹם אֶחָד לָעֹמֶר:

Let's keep the planet beautiful. Today, try to pick up some litter or trash from the ground. What are some common examples of trash you may find on the ground? List some below.

○ I counted up today!

Day 37

כ"ב אייר

Today is Thirty-Seven Days, which are Five Weeks and Two Days of the Omer.

הַיּוֹם שִׁבְעָה וּשְׁלֹשִׁים יוֹם,
שֶׁהֵם חֲמִשָּׁה שָׁבוּעוֹת
וּשְׁנֵי יָמִים לָעֹמֶר:

One way to take care of our world is by planting more. Today, plant a plant, tree, or flower. (Or, if you can't do that, donate to an organization that cares for the earth.) Draw some flowers and trees below.

 I counted up today!

Day 38

כ"ג אייר

Today is Thirty-Eight
Days, which are Five
Weeks and Three
Days of the Omer.

הַיּוֹם שְׁמוֹנָה וּשְׁלֹשִׁים
יוֹם, שֶׁהֵם חֲמִשָּׁה
שָׁבוּעוֹת וּשְׁלֹשָׁה יָמִים
לָעֹמֶר:

Caring for animals is a Jewish value. Today, put out some
water or seeds for the birds. And then enjoy watching from
afar as birds have the refreshments. In the space below,
draw a bird enjoying a snack.

I counted up today!

Day 39

Today is Thirty-Nine Days, which are Five Weeks and Four Days of the Omer.

הַיּוֹם תִּשְׁעָה וּשְׁלֹשִׁים יוֹם, שֶׁהֵם חֲמִשָּׁה שָׁבוּעוֹת וְאַרְבָּעָה יָמִים לָעֹמֶר:

Today, think about ways to reduce the amount of electricity you use. Unplug what you're not using, turn the lights off when you leave a room, and spend more time outside. Below, list examples of when you use electricity in your day-to-day life.

 I counted up today!

Day 40

Today is Forty Days, which are Five Weeks and Five Days of the Omer.

הַיּוֹם אַרְבָּעִים יוֹם, שֶׁהֵם חֲמִשָּׁה שָׁבוּעוֹת וַחֲמִשָּׁה יָמִים לָעֹמֶר:

We can prevent car pollution by walking and bike-riding more. Even carpooling can help. How can you help reduce car pollution today? Jot down some ideas below, and then choose one to do.

 I counted up today!

Day 41

Today is Forty-One
Days, which are Five
Weeks and Six Days
of the Omer.

הַיּוֹם אֶחָד וְאַרְבָּעִים יוֹם,
שֶׁהֵם חֲמִשָּׁה שָׁבוּעוֹת
וְשִׁשָּׁה יָמִים לָעֹמֶר:

Today, let's think about conserving water. What are some
ways you can use less? For example, you can shut off the
water while brushing your teeth or take a shorter shower.
Jot down or draw some ideas below.

 I counted up today!

Day 42

Today is Forty-Two
Days, which are Six
Weeks of the Omer.

הַיּוֹם שְׁנַיִם וְאַרְבָּעִים
יוֹם, שֶׁהֵם שִׁשָּׁה שָׁבוּעוֹת
לָעֹמֶר:

We, humans, create a lot of garbage. Today, your challenge is to limit your trash waste. For example, use reusable containers and a reusable water bottle. Below, jot down some of the items you throw out most often, and then think of ways you can reduce that today.

 I counted up today!

Week 6:
Time to Reflect

Flip back and skim the pages from this past week. What were your highlights? What was the biggest challenge? What do you hope to bring with you into the future weeks? Jot down some thoughts below.

Week 7

Look all around
for kindness.

This is the last week of the *Omer*, and it's a great time to reflect on kindness and look back at your growth these past several weeks.

Day 43

Yom Yerushalayim   כ״ח אייר

Today is Forty-Three Days, which are Six Weeks and One Day of the Omer.

הַיּוֹם שְׁלֹשָׁה וְאַרְבָּעִים יוֹם, שֶׁהֵם שִׁשָּׁה שָׁבוּעוֹת וְיוֹם אֶחָד לָעֹמֶר:

Think about a favorite story of yours that you've read, heard, or watched. What is an inspiring act of kindness in that story? Write about it or draw it below.

 I counted up today!

Day 44

Today is Forty-Four Days, which are Six Weeks and Two Days of the Omer.

הַיּוֹם אַרְבָּעָה וְאַרְבָּעִים יוֹם, שֶׁהֵם שִׁשָּׁה שָׁבוּעוֹת וּשְׁנֵי יָמִים לָעֹמֶר:

Did someone do something kind for you today? It can be a small or big act of kindness. Write about it or draw a picture of it below.

 I counted up today!

Day 45

Rosh Chodesh

א׳ סיון

Today is Forty-Five
Days, which are Six
Weeks and Three
Days of the Omer.

הַיּוֹם חֲמִשָּׁה וְאַרְבָּעִים
יוֹם, שֶׁהֵם שִׁשָּׁה שָׁבוּעוֹת
וּשְׁלֹשָׁה יָמִים לָעֹמֶר:

Looking back on your past, what is a major act of kindness
that someone did for you? Write about it or draw a picture
of it below.

 I counted up today!

Day 46

Today is Forty-Six
Days, which are Six
Weeks and Four Days
of the Omer.

הַיּוֹם שִׁשָּׁה וְאַרְבָּעִים
יוֹם, שֶׁהֵם שִׁשָּׁה שָׁבוּעוֹת
וְאַרְבָּעָה יָמִים לָעֹמֶר:

Imagine you had unlimited money to do an act of kindness.
What is something kind you dream of doing someday?

I counted up today!

Day 47

Today is Forty-Seven Days, which are Six Weeks and Five Days of the Omer.

הַיּוֹם שִׁבְעָה וְאַרְבָּעִים יוֹם, שֶׁהֵם שִׁשָּׁה שָׁבוּעוֹת וַחֲמִשָּׁה יָמִים לָעֹמֶר:

Looking back at the last several weeks, what is an act of kindness you did that you especially enjoyed? Write about it or draw a picture of it below.

 I counted up today!

Day 48

Today is Forty-Eight
Days, which are Six
Weeks and Six Days
of the Omer.

הַיּוֹם שְׁמוֹנָה וְאַרְבָּעִים
יוֹם, שֶׁהֵם שִׁשָּׁה שָׁבוּעוֹת
וְשִׁשָּׁה יָמִים לָעֹמֶר:

If you could design a billboard asking people to do more
kindness, what would you write on it? Design your billboard
below.

 I counted up today!

Day 49

Today is Forty-Nine Days, which are Seven Weeks of the Omer.

הַיּוֹם תִּשְׁעָה וְאַרְבָּעִים יוֹם, שֶׁהֵם שִׁבְעָה שָׁבוּעוֹת לָעֹמֶר:

Have you changed at all, as a person, this *Omer*? Describe it below, in words or pictures.

 I counted up today!

Week 7:
Time to Reflect

Flip back and skim the pages from this past week. What were your highlights? What was the biggest challenge? What do you hope to bring with you into the future weeks? Jot down some thoughts below.

Yay!

Now it's time to celebrate! Why? You counted the seven weeks of the *Omer*. And, throughout the process, you became a kinder person.

Treat yourself to something fun and take some time to feel good about your progress. You made the world a kinder place.

Cut the certificate out on the next page. Fill it out and hang it somewhere special.

Chag Sameach!

The Official Counting Up Certificate

Presented to

_____

for counting the days and making the days count.

Signed,

Sari Kopitnikoff

About the Author

Sari is an experiential educator, digital artist, educational performer, and content creator. She is passionate about creating books, games, activities, shows, virtual challenges, and interactive workshops that bring Judaism to life.

You can follow Sari's work on Instagram, Facebook, and TikTok @ThatJewishMoment, and you can find lots of free Jewish educational materials at ThatJewishMoment.com. There, you can arrange for Sari to give a live or virtual workshop, sign up for her newsletter, or just say hi.

Other books by Sari:

That Jewish Moment
My Davening Diary
Jewmagine That!
My Escape from Egypt
Only Kidding!

Made in United States
North Haven, CT
18 April 2023

35605455R00046